Let's Talk About Hell

by

Kenneth N. Myers

Let's Talk About Hell

© Copyright 2021 by Kenneth N. Myers
All rights reserved
This book or parts thereof may not be reproduced in any form, stored in a retrieval system, or transmitted in any form by any means - electronic, mechanical, photocopy, recording or otherwise - without prior written permission of the publisher, except as provided by United States of America copyright law.

Unless otherwise indicated, Scripture quotations are from The Holy Bible, English Standard Version® (ESV®), copyright © 2001 by Crossway, a publishing ministry of Good News Publishers. Used by permission. All rights reserved.

Myers, Kenneth Neal, 1959-
Let's Talk About Hell/Kenneth N. Myers

Cover design: Michael Peterson

Published by Mayeux Press
561 Bailey Drive, Denison TX 75021

Mayeux Press
DENISON, TEXAS

For my son Jay,
who got here before I did;

for Alayne,
who made me answer the question;

and for Tommy,
who is kind to strangers.

A special thank you to Deacon Mat and Kristina Allen, Fr. Jim Curry, Rae Dickson, and Sheila Moore for their insights and help.

Table of Content

	Forward	7
Chapter 1	It All Depends On What You Mean By…	11
Chapter 2	Let's Talk About God	31
Chapter 3	Let's Talk About God Some More	43
Chapter 4	What Even Does Hell Mean?	53
Chapter 5	The Apostles	73
Chapter 6	What Jesus Said About Hell	81
Chapter 7	Eternal Fire	101
Chapter 8	Avoiding The Flames	113
Chapter 9	Jesus Saves	127
	Notable Christians Who Held This Hope	135
	Suggested Reading	141

Foreword

Eight years ago I wrote a book titled, *Salvation And How We Got It Wrong*, and have taught seminars on it all over America. I have received letters from atheists who came to Christ after reading the book. I have received phone calls and messages from people all around the world who read it and told me it changed their lives and expanded their awe in who Christ is and what he has accomplished for us.

Without fail, although the subject is never even approached in the seminars, someone in the audience will ask, "Well, what about hell?" I usually try to skirt the issue and say something like, "Well, that's not the subject of this seminar!" When I was teaching the seminar at a church in Florida, true to form during the question and answer time, someone asked, "Well, what about hell?" I skirted the issue. Another hand went up, "Ok, but, what about hell?" I skirted it again. Then a third hand went up. It was the wife of the local priest and a formidable student of theology herself. "But, what about hell?" It was less a question and more a matter of fact demand for an explanation. So I taught a half hour overview, shooting from the hip, without notes, on an ancient doctrine held by many notable Christians that the fire of hell was actually cleansing, not torturing.

Since then, when the question comes up, as often as not I will give that same little off the cuff teaching. People's responses range from, "I sure *wish* that was true, but I don't know if I can believe it," to, "Oh, my! This really *is* Good News!"

And then people began telling me I should write a book on the subject. Let me say this: there are already a lot of good books that address this hopeful view of hell (and I will list some of them in the Suggested Reading appendix). But after this little half hour teaching developed into a well researched series, I have finally put it on paper. What follows is not thinking outside the box; it is just making the box a lot bigger.

I have joked that if I ever wrote a book on hell, it ought to be the last thing I write, right before I die, because there was a good chance I would get blacklisted, or burned at the stake. Well, I hope I don't die anytime soon, and I hope I don't get blacklisted or burned at the stake. We shall see. Here is the book.

Chapter One

It All Depends On What You Mean By...

"Well, I don't give one iota..." I can still hear my north Texas farmer grandfather saying that with a note of disdain in his voice. Not giving one iota meant not caring one little bit. He didn't give one iota about politics. Or about geography. Or history. Or much anything of learning. With a third grade education, his priorities were making a living for his family, caring for a little farm, and watching professional wrestling. When I was a young boy he took me to the Dallas Sportatoreum where we watched Fritz Von Erich barely defeat Pretty Boy George. When it got particularly intense and Von Erich slammed George to the mat, my grandpa leaned over and emphatically said, "Now, don't tell me *that's* fake!" I came home raving about it to my parents. They didn't give one iota.

One Iota

The phrase, "I don't give one iota" has a fascinating history. In the very first major church council, the Council of Nicaea in 325, the major disagreement concerned defining how Jesus related to God the Father. The orthodox leaders insisted that God the Son was, "of the same substance" as God the Father; the Father and Son were one. The opposing clergy, led by a fellow named Arius, insisted that the Son was in fact *not* of the same substance as the Father, but rather of, "a similar substance." The orthodox were saying Jesus is God come in the flesh, the heterodox were saying the Son is like God, but he isn't God; he is a creation, and there was a time when he was not.

This is a huge theological issue. I mean, honestly, the hugest! But watch this. The two Greek words translated "same substance" and "similar substance" are different by only one letter. Yep, you guessed it: that letter is the smallest in the Greek alphabet, the Greek "i", iota! If you give one iota, *homoousios* becomes *homoiousios*, and Jesus becomes just a godly man, not the God Man. But the orthodox leaders wouldn't give one iota.

If you are part of a liturgical church, then you are familiar with and regularly confess what came out of the council:

> I believe in one Lord Jesus Christ,
> the Only Begotten Son of God,
> begotten of his Father before all ages,

> God of God, Light of Light,
> very God of very God,
> begotten, not made,
> being of one substance with the Father;
> by whom all things were made…

Sometimes a lot hangs on a little thing, and sometimes definitions are important.

It All Depends On What You Mean By…

When people ask me if I believe in XYZ, I always ask them to first define XYZ before I give my answer. "Do you believe in Jesus?" Well, that depends. What do you mean by *believe*, and who do you mean by *Jesus*?

If Jesus refers to the guy selling tacos from the food truck, and believe means to put my trust and faith in him, then, no, I don't believe in Jesus. I mean, he might be a great guy, but I don't even really know him.

I just like his tacos. But to be honest, my friend Victor makes much better tacos.

If Jesus refers to the Jehovah's Witnesses' or Mormons' understanding of the son of Mary who was born in Bethlehem 2,000 years ago, then again, no, I don't believe in Jesus. Not that Jesus. That Jesus is human and not divine, not the one true God come in the flesh. I don't believe in that Jesus. So I'd have to answer no.

We live in an era when the meaning of words is as perceived by the hearer, and I guess that's OK on some level, but definitions are of major importance if we are going to actually communicate with one another. As a young boy I remember being disappointed to the point of tears because my dad asked me if I wanted a Coke and I said yes and the waitress brought me a Coke when I was expecting an orange soda. To my mind, Coke meant any kind of soft drink, and it really meant an, "orange Coke." If we don't understand each other's definitions, then we aren't going to understand each other's words. The more important the subject being discussed, the more true this is. Sometimes the most important question we can ask is, "What do you mean by that?"

Do I believe in Jesus? If by believe you mean put my trust and confidence in and pledge my allegiance to, and if by Jesus you mean God the Son, eternally begotten of the Father and born of the Virgin Mary, who was crucified, died, was buried, descended into Hades, rose again, ascended into heaven, and is coming again on the last day to make right all things, then, yes, I believe in Jesus.

Now, ask me if I believe in hell.

The Bad Thing About Hell

When it comes to talking about hell, once again it is important to ask, "What do you mean by hell?" When one person uses the word she may mean a spiritual state of painful separation from God. When someone else uses the word, he may mean a literal place of physical fire and darkness where God sends people who didn't receive Christ as their personal lord and savior, where they will be tortured for all eternity, world without end, amen. When someone else says the word, they may indeed be referring to the lovely village in Norway.

The bad thing about hell is that in most English translations of the Bible, it is a catch-all word used to translate several different Hebrew and Greek words with very different meanings.

"When you are at the store, get me a bag of flour." Easy enough. But wait - what kind of flour? Rice flour, bread flour, self-rising flour, buckwheat flour, all-purpose flour, almond flour, whole wheat flour? That's confusing enough, but what if we also throw in, under the various definitions of flour, something like, oh, say, corn meal?

Or maybe, bananas? "That's absurd," you say, and you are correct. Corn meal isn't flour (even if you can argue for a certain similarity), and bananas are absolutely not flour!

Well, I'm here to tell you that using "hell" as a catch-word for all kinds of different Hebrew and Greek words is equally as absurd. *Sheol, Hades, Genenna,* and *Tartarus* are not the same thing (more about each of these words later). Not even close. Some of them are as different from one another as buckwheat is from bananas. But they all get lumped into the same English word. Hell if I know why (I had to do that just once in this book. Now that I have it out of my system, please proceed).

"Do you believe in hell?" Do you mean a literal hell, a spiritual hell, a figurative hell, a physical hell, a symbolic hell?

Three Views of Hell

Hell is one of those subjects that some people use to determine whether you are a real Christian. Some people think that if you don't believe what they believe about hell, then you are a heretic, don't believe the Bible, are likely not saved, and are probably going to hell (I mean, to *their* version of hell).

But the reality is there are different understandings of hell that have always existed in the Church and have been within the realm of orthodox Christian faith. The dominance of these views has ebbed and flowed throughout history and across various Christian movements. What was believed by early Christians in Egypt, for example, is decidedly different from what is believed today by most Christians in Texas. Depending on when and where you lived, you may have held a different view of hell than what is popularly held in much of Western Christianity now. But that wouldn't have made you a heretic or somehow less of a Christian. So, here are the three ways of understanding hell.

1: The Fire That Torments

Eternal Conscious Torment. ECT for short. This is the most common understanding of hell in Western Christianity today, and it is largely due to the influence of the fourth/fifth century non-Greek and non-Hebrew reading Saint Augustine (a man of stellar brilliance who also got some things wrong). Early in his ministry Augustine didn't give much thought to the question of hell, but later, and under the influence of St. Jerome, whose Latin translation of the Bible, the *Vulgate*, uses the word *infernum* 110 times (the first major case of mistranslating *sheol, hades, genenna,* and *tartarus* all as "hell"), he developed a vigorous doctrine of hell, insisting that it was a place of unrelenting torment. Augustine saw it as a place of literal fire where the unredeemed in their immortal, physical, resurrected bodies would burn forever, with limbs burning away and then reappearing, only to be burned away again, not for a thousand years, not for a million years, but for eternity.

Augustine recognized that a great many, even most, Christians of his time did not believe in eternal conscious torment. Even though he thought them wrong (because they desired to be soft and merciful), he did not reject them as not being Christians or as heretical; he even wrote that they did not, "go counter to divine Scripture."[1] In fact, he yielded to their way ever so slightly, saying it was OK to think that even if this torment was eternal, there might well be times when God in his mercy would give the tormented a little relief:

---

[1] Augustine, *Enchiridion*, 29.112.

> "But let them suppose, if it pleases them, that, for certain intervals of time, the punishments of the damned are somewhat mitigated. Even so, the wrath of God must be understood as still resting on them…Yet even in his wrath - his wrath resting on them - he does not 'shut up his mercy.' This is not to put an end to their eternal afflictions, but rather to apply or interpose some little respite in their torments."[2]

Augustine became the most influential theologian in the Roman Catholic Church, and Martin Luther, as a former Augustinian monk, brought his influence into Protestantism as well.

In medieval Catholicism, including in popular plays of the time, this view of hell took center stage; it became a primary focus of popular Christian thinking, the theme of a great many sermons, the terrifying subject of traveling staged

---

[2] *ibid.*

dramas, and the stuff used by the 14th century Italian poet Dante Alighieri to build his poem *Inferno*, which consequently served as the most influential depiction of hell for the next seven centuries. In fact, a lot of what many modern Christians think the Bible teaches about hell is actually from Dante's poem.

The Eternal Conscious Torment doctrine jumped the tracks into Evangelicalism as well and served as the terrifying focus of most evangelistic sermons throughout the 19th and 20th centuries.

Consequently, Augustine's view of hell is most likely the view you were taught as a child, wrestled with in later years, and either accept or reject now. It may be the view which you hold so tightly that you assume others who think differently are unquestionably off track and possibly heretical. Or it may be the view you hold ever so gingerly, because you think you must in order to be a real Christian. And, whether it is correct or incorrect, it is a view that has caused many people to walk away from Christianity entirely.

This book is not about this view.

2. The Fire That Destroys

The second view of hell held within orthodox Christianity is called annihilationism or conditional immortality: the understanding that in the end, God simply destroys the wicked, and they cease to exist. This belief was held by some early Christian thinkers such as Arnobius and hinted at by others (including Iraneaus).

While never a majority doctrine in early Christianity, it was present then, and there continues a stream of Christians who hold to this teaching today, including modern Evangelical and Anglican scholars such as Clark Pinnock, Philip Edgecumbe Hughes, and John Stott. The basic idea is that at some point in the afterlife, God in his mercy simply terminates the very existence of the wicked. They cease to be. They are not tormented forever, they are consumed in the fire of judgment.

This book is not about this view.

3. The Fire That Cleanses

The third way of understanding hell has many different labels, but for the sake of clarity we will call it purgatorial universal reconciliation, or PUR for short. Held by a great many notable Early Church Fathers, many modern Eastern Orthodox theologians, a thread of Protestant thinkers throughout history, and heavily leaned toward by some modern Roman Catholic theologians, this view holds the purpose of the fire of hell is not to torture, nor to destroy, rather, like a "refiner's fire," to purify, and that, indeed, this is the very presence of God himself. "Our God is a consuming fire," the writer of Hebrews tells us (12.29). Those who hold to this understanding of hell believe that the consuming fire that is God himself will burn away everything - every sin, every wrong, every evil within the human heart - which keeps a person from being fully united with him.

Held by such early Christian leaders as St. Gregory of Nyssa (who presided at the Council of Constantinople in 381 and penned the final section of the Nicene Creed), Clement of Alexandria, Origen, Dionysius of Alexandria, Evagrius, Isaac of Ninevah, St. Symeon the New Theologian, and many others, this was the dominant understanding before Augustine stepped onto the stage of Christian history.

Although it never completely disappeared, the purgatorial universal reconciliation view of hell became so insignificant in later Western Christianity that those who embrace it in modern history have been held suspect and even considered heretical. An example is the

Scottish theologian, pastor and writer George MacDonald (1824-1905).

MacDonald had an enormous influence on C.S. Lewis (although he died before Lewis was aware of him) and Lewis referred to MacDonald as, "my master." Lewis even has him as a central character in his novel about heaven and hell, *The Great Divorce*), is greatly loved by generations of Evangelicals for his Christian fairy tales and children's stories, yet is also kept at arm's length by them because of his view of eternity.

The PUR stream has always been stronger in Eastern Orthodoxy, and has had a resurgence in modern times including in the writings of Metropolitan Kallistos Ware of Diokleia, and Archbishop Hilarion Alfayev of Moscow. In the Roman Catholic Church we find it in the theology of Pope St. John Paul II's favorite theologian, Hans Urs Von Balthasar. It should be noted that none of these approach the subject with dogmatism, rather that as Christians we may (even must) *hope* that all people will be saved.

In the Anglican world, this view has been embraced by William Law, Thomas Allin, F.W. Farrar, John A.T. Robinson, the popular novelist Madeleine L'Engle, and others. C.S. Lewis would be considered a "hopeful universalist," writing that "hell's doors are locked from the inside." It has also been, and is still, strongly rejected among many Anglicans.

Protestantism in general has been particularly closed to the notion that the purpose of hell is purification. But even in this camp it is making a resurgence in our own time.

Purgatorial universal reconciliation, "hopeful universalism," and similar views of hell focus not only on the teachings of Scripture regarding the immediate subject of hell, but also on the nature and character of God himself. This view begins with the understanding that God is love, that Jesus himself is the pure and exact representation of the heart of God, and that the popular eternal conscious torment view of hell is inconsistent with who God is.

This book is about this view.

Chapter Two

Let's Talk About God

God is the starting place for everything. Literally! And God is the starting place for us to discuss hell, because, whatever hell is, God created it. If hell is a place of eternal conscious torment, it is so by the will and purpose of God. Likewise if hell is a place of destroying, soul-ending flames, God made it so. And if hell is a place of purifying fire, well, that too finds its source in God. So, before we talk about hell itself, let's talk about the One who made it.

The Bible teaches us certain things about the nature and character of God, or the "attributes" of God; things like God is uncreated, God is omnipotent, God is omniscient. There are four attributes of God that are important for us to consider before we look at the biblical doctrine of hell itself.

God is Love

The Apostle John wrote, "Anyone who does not love does not know God, because God is love." (1 John 4.8) Whatever else we say about God, this is foundational. Love isn't something God possesses: John doesn't say God "has" love, but that God *is* love. Everything that flows from God flows from love. There are four words in Greek translated into English with the single word love, each with a special nuance. The word John uses here is *agape*, which is the highest kind of love, not rooted in emotion, or familial relationship, or romance, or friendship, but rooted in goodness; rooted in seeking the other's highest good. It is a selfless and self-giving kind of love; a sacrificial love. "For God so loved the world," John wrote, "that he gave his only Son that whoever believes in him should not perish but have eternal life." (John 3.16) In the pagan religions of the past, people sacrificed *others* in order to appease their angry gods. In Christianity, God sacrifices *himself* to reconcile the world to himself: God is love.

Whether hell is a place of eternal torment or cleansing fire, we must agree it is created by the God who is himself self giving, self sacrificing love.

God is Merciful

"Most merciful God…" So begin many of our prayers. The wonderful Anglican Prayer of Humble Access includes the line, "but thou art the same Lord whose property is always to have mercy…" St.

Paul calls God, "the Father of mercies" (2 Corinthians 1.3), and St. James tells us, "the Lord is compassionate and merciful." (James 5.11). Is God just? Of course he is, but even more, he is merciful. If God were purely justice, without compassion or mercy, we would all be without hope, for it would never have been in his heart to send Christ into the world to save us. The incarnation itself, and the death of Christ, are remarkable and bold revelations of the merciful heart of God. His property is *always* to have mercy.

Whether hell is a place of eternal torment or cleansing fire, we must agree it is created by a merciful God.

God Is Forgiving

Moses encountered God in the flaming bush in the desert, but didn't know who God was. "What is your name," Moses asked, and God said, "I Am." Later, Moses yearned to know God more; to see him. God told him that he couldn't see him, that in fact, no human could look upon the sheer power of his naked glory and survive. But, God made a deal with Moses. He told him that he would set Moses in the cleft of a rock, a big crevice in the side of a mountain, and when God passed before him, he would let Moses see the "backside" of his glory. Exodus tells us the rest of the story:

> The Lord descended in the cloud and stood with him there, and proclaimed the name of the Lord. The Lord passed before him and proclaimed, "The Lord, the Lord, a God *merciful and gracious, slow to anger, and abounding in steadfast love and faithfulness, keeping steadfast love for thousands, forgiving iniquity and transgression and sin,* but who will by no means clear the guilty, visiting the iniquity of the fathers on the children and the children's children, to the third and the fourth generation." (Exodus 34.5-7)

Does it not inform our view of hell that when God revealed himself to Moses as much as Moses could handle, he described himself as being merciful, gracious, slow to anger, overflowing in love, overflowing in faithfulness, and having a heart of forgiveness for sin? God could have painted a much different picture. He could have painted the same picture that too many Christians over the years have painted: that God is *primarily* a God of judgment, condemnation, and scorekeeping. He goes on to make it clear that there are consequences for our sins - "he will by no means clear the guilty" - but the punishment of God is corrective, not simply vengeful. It serves a purpose that is not contrary to mercy, grace, love, faithfulness, and forgiveness, rather it is an outflow of these things. Because God loves us, is faithful to us, is merciful to us, he corrects us, for our own good, and for the good of all. "For the Lord disciplines the one he loves, and chastises every son whom he receives" (Hebrews 12.6) But in all cases, when God punishes, it is the self-sacrificing Agape Love himself correcting us, not some angry and almighty potentate insisting on getting his pound of flesh.

Whether hell is a place of eternal torment or cleansing fire, we must agree it is created by a forgiving God.

God Is Unchanging

The pagan gods of the ancient world were as fickle as opportunistic politicians. You never knew where they stood, or what mood they would be in. That's why you walked softly around them, tried to not anger them, and were willing to make whatever sacrifices they demanded, even to the point of burning your own children, in order to curry their favor.

In the story of Abraham offering his son Isaac, we see not only a foreshadowing of God offering his own Son, but we also see that Judaism *begins* with the abolition of human sacrifice. Abraham was willing to offer his son, because that's what his people did back home. Human sacrifices sound abhorrent to us, but they were run of the mill in Abraham's culture. God wants me to sacrifice my son for him, Abraham thinks, no big surprise there. So Abraham heads to the hills with Isaac, some firewood, and a big knife, and is ready to do the deed. Then God stops him. As if to say, "Abe, that may be how your ancestors do it back home, but I'm not the God of your ancestors. I'm not the God demanding human blood. We'll have none of that here." The only times afterward that the people of Abraham fell into human sacrifice was when they fell away from Yahweh and turned to other gods.

Unlike the pagan gods, our God is not fickle. He is not wishy-washy. He is not always changing. In fact, the Bible repeatedly gives the important truth that God, the *real* God, is changeless. "God is not man, that he should lie, nor a son of man, *that he should change his mind.* Has he said, and will he not do it? Or has he spoken, and will he not fulfill it?" (Numbers 23.19)

One of the great joys in the Judeo-Christian understanding of God is that we can trust him, and we can trust him because he is "faithful" or "trustworthy," or to put it another way, he is dependable. And he is dependable because he doesn't change every other day. "For I the Lord *do not change*; therefore you, O children of Jacob, are not consumed." (Malachi 3.6).

In light of this, when the writer of Hebrews describes our confidence in Jesus, he writes, "Jesus Christ is *the same yesterday and today and forever.*" (Hebrews 13.8)

My point is that God doesn't change. He isn't loving and forgiving one day, and then unmerciful and unforgiving the next. We change. Things change. Times change. God doesn't change. His "property is to always have mercy."

Whether hell is a place of eternal torment or cleansing fire, we must agree it is created by an unchanging God.

Jesus Is The Best Picture Of God

When the writer of Hebrews begins his letter, he describes Jesus as, "…the radiance of the glory of God and *the exact imprint of his nature*…" (Hebrews 1.3) Christianity is careful to point out that there are not thousands of Gods. There are not even three Gods (Father, Son, and Holy Spirit). There is one God, and that one God is revealed fully and exactly in the person of Jesus Christ. In other words, if you want to know what this loving, merciful, forgiving, unchanging God is really like, look at Jesus. God is *exactly* like Jesus, because Jesus *is* God come in the flesh.

When the disciple Philip came to Jesus and asked him to show them the Father,

Jesus replied (I'm convinced he slapped himself on the forehead right before he said this), "Have I been with you so long, and you still do not know me, Philip? *Whoever has seen me has seen the Father.*" (John 14.9)

There is no juxtaposition between the Father and the Son (or the Holy Spirit). There is no "good God/bad God" scenario going on here. There is no, "God the Father is harsh and tormenting, but God the Son is loving and forgiving." There is no Son saving us from the Father. The Son saves us from sin and death, not from the Father; the Father loves us. There is one God, and he is fully revealed in the person of Jesus Christ. Indeed, the Bible teaches that it was through the Son that *everything* was created and has its being (Hebrews 1.2).

Whether hell is a place of eternal torment or cleansing fire, we must agree it is created by Jesus.

Chapter Three

Let's Talk About God Some More

People get their perceptions about God from a lot of different places. From hymns, and movies, and friends, and books, and even from their relationship with their own earthly father. But I would wager that the majority of church going people arrive at their understanding about God primarily from the influence of sermons.

In some current circles there is no sermonic focus on the nature of God. Instead the preachers focus on getting ahead in life, being successful, and having lots of money. I suppose even this communicates something about God, leaving the hearer with the impression that God is a kind of cosmic Santa Claus whose primary purpose is to give us our best life now. In other circles the preachers paint a portrait of God that is downright terrifying: God's primary disposition toward us is one of wrath; he is keeping score and just waiting to deal out retribution; his first inclination toward a fallen creation is hatred. Unfortunately, this view crosses denominational lines. People can hear it in churches as divergent as Catholic, Presbyterian, Pentecostal, Baptist, Methodist, Anglican and anything in between.

In the last chapter we talked about the characteristics of God. We saw that he is full of mercy, forgiving, loving, and unchanging. In this chapter we are going to look at what the Bible reveals about God's disposition toward his creation, and particularly, toward humanity, that pinnacle of creation made in his image.

Some Verses To Ponder

You know how sometimes when you are reading a book and it quotes several Bible verses you kind of just scan those texts and hurry on, because you are already familiar with the scriptures noted? Well, don't do that in this chapter. Please take the time to read the biblical texts printed below. Read them slowly, or at least don't hurry through them. And *ponder* them as you read. Ruminate. Meditate. Contemplate. You get the idea. As you read, ask yourself the question, "What do these texts tell me about God's attitude, his heart, his disposition toward me, toward humankind, and toward all of creation?" While you are at it, also ask this: "What is the scope of God's redemptive plan? Just how big and wide is it?"

For the rest of this short chapter, I'm just going to let the Bible speak for itself. Ready? Let's do this.

- Lamentations 3.22-23; 31-32: The **steadfast love** of the Lord **never ceases**; his **mercies never come to an end**; they are new every morning, **great is your faithfulness**…For the Lord will not cast off forever, but, though he cause grief, he will have **compassion** according to the **abundance of his steadfast love**.

- Wisdom 11.23-12.2: But you are merciful to **all**, for you can do all things, and you **overlook people's sins**, so that they may repent. For you **love all things that exist**, and **detest none of the things that you have made**, for you would not have made anything if you had hated it. How would anything have endured if you had not willed it? Or how would anything not called forth by you have been preserved? **You spare all things**, for they are yours, O Lord, you who **love the living**. For

your immortal spirit is in all things.
Therefore **you correct little by little** those
who trespass, and you remind and warn
them of the things through which they
sin, so that they may be freed from
wickedness and put their trust in you, O
Lord.

- Mt. 17.10-11: And the disciples asked him,
  "Then why do the scribes say that first
  Elijah must come?" He answered, "Elijah
  does come, and he will **restore all
  things**."

- John 1.29: The next day he [John the
  Baptist] saw Jesus coming toward him,
  and said, "Behold, the Lamb of God,
  who **takes away the sin of the world!**"

- John 3.16-17: For God so **loved** the world,
  that he gave his only Son, that whoever
  believes in him should not perish but
  have eternal life. For God did not send his
  Son into the world to condemn the world,
  but in order that **the world might be
  saved** through him.

- John 12.32: And I, when I am lifted up from the earth, will draw **all people** to myself.

- John. 12.47: If anyone hears my words and does not keep them, I do not judge him; for I did not come to judge the world but to **save the world.**

- John. 17.1-2: After Jesus had spoken these words, he looked up to heaven and said, "Father, the hour has come; glorify your Son so that the Son may glorify you, since you have given him authority over **all people**, to give eternal life to **all** whom you have given him.

- Acts 3,19-21 (NRSV): Repent therefore, and turn to God so that your sins may be wiped out, so that times of refreshing may come from the presence of the Lord, and that he may send the Messiah appointed for you, that is, Jesus, who must remain in heaven until the time of **universal restoration** [*apokatastaseos* *panton*; "restoration of all"] that God announced long ago through his holy prophets.

- Romans 3.23-24: for **all have sinned** and fall short of the glory of God, **and are justified by his grace** as a gift, through the redemption that is in Christ Jesus

- Romans 11.32: For God has consigned all to disobedience, that he may **have mercy on all.**

- 1 Corinthians 15.22: For as in Adam all die, so also in Christ shall **all be made alive.**

- 2 Corinthians 5.19: in Christ God was **reconciling the world** to himself, **not counting their trespasses** against them, and entrusting to us the message of reconciliation.

- Colossians 1.19-20: For in him all the fullness of God was pleased to dwell, and through him to reconcile to himself **all**

things, whether on earth or in heaven, making peace by the blood of his cross.

- 1 Timothy 2.3-4: This is good, and it is pleasing in the sight of God our Savior, who desires **all people** to be saved and to come to the knowledge of the truth.

- 1 Timothy 4.10: to this end we toil and strive, because we have our hope set on the living God, **who is the Savior of all people**, especially of those who believe.

- 1 John 2.2: He is the propitiation for our sins, and not for ours only but also for the sins of **the whole world**.

- 1 John 4.14: And we have seen and do testify that the Father has sent his Son as the **Savior of the world**.

These verses reveal a God unlike the one declared from many pulpits. God's primary inclination is toward reconciliation. His heart is to step in where things are broken and repair them, to enter a world that has fallen and to lift it up, to reach into the depths of despair and bring rescue.

In light of this ask yourself one more question: "Knowing what we know about the heart of God, which of the three views of hell is best aligned to God himself?" Clearly, this question alone isn't the determining factor of our doctrine of hell, but it is a good question to ask and to contemplate.

Chapter Four

What Even Does Hell Mean?

Robert Capon wrote that words are like train cars: they carry different cargo at different times. A car carrying corn on one trip may carry wheat on another. Words sometimes carry a different cargo of meaning. Take, for example, the word "world." In John 3.16 we read, "For God so loved the world…" But in 1 John 2.15 the same writer tells us, "Do not love the world or the things in the world. If anyone loves the world, the love of the Father is not in him." Clearly "world" means two different things in these texts. In the first reference world means the created realm, in the second, the connotation is "worldliness," the fallen system that is contrary to the things of God. And yet, both use the same word - world - to describe these very different things. This is why it is important to dig down, to research, to compare, and to actually *think* about what we are reading in the Bible.

When it comes to the word hell, meanings become even more complicated, because the English word itself is actually borrowed from the Old Norse *hel.* In Norse mythology, *Hel* is the name of the god Loki's daughter, who rules over the misty underworld where evil souls are kept; the place also takes her name, so the Norse called the underworld *hel.*

As an aside, imagine a Christian missionary trying to describe heaven and hell to a group of Vikings, using their own language - *Valhalla* and *Hel*. What gets painted in the minds of the Vikings is not some pure Christian teaching, rather whatever the missionary is telling them, colored by their own preconceived versions of the places those words represent. Now, imagine that those Vikings do in fact convert to Christianity, and the missionary teaches them the rudiments of the faith then goes on to the next village. What do those Vikings teach their children and grandchildren about heaven and hell?

So, the pagan Angles and Saxons rob the Old Norse of its word for the misty underworld ruled by Loki's daughter, and bring it over into their emerging new language, English. Then they become Christians and keep using the word to translate different biblical words that don't all mean the same thing.

Here, then, is the very first use of the Old Norse *hel* in an English translation of the Bible. Numbers 16.30 in the Tyndale Bible (1530):

> But and yf the Lorde make a newe thinge and the erth open hir mouthe and swalowe them and all that pertayne vnto them so that they goo doune quycke in to **hell**: then ye shall vnderstod that these me haue rayled apon the Lorde.

Do you see how a word is like a train car? By the time Tyndale uses the word in his Bible, its cargo is a mixture of Greek mythology (more on this momentarily), Norse mythology, Jewish tradition, Latin influence, and Christian thinking. Add to this all the different images of hell painted by zealous preachers over the years and it is no wonder there is confusion and misinformation about hell in the 21st century.

Say the word hell and one person imagines a place of relentless fire and unending agony; someone else imagines a place of darkness and silence and the absence of God's presence; someone else imagines something completely different.

For the moment, let's go with the popular definition of hell: a place of unending torment to which God banishes people for eternity. What, then, does the Bible actually say about hell?

The Old Testament

Nothing. Nada. Zero. Zip. The Old Testament doesn't teach us *anything* about hell. Shocking, I know! I mean, if this underworld torture chamber was actually created by God as part of his grand design for the universe and eternity, wouldn't it be part of the description of creation in Genesis? Wouldn't it be a significant omission for the Holy Spirit inspired writers of the first book of the Bible to omit such an important aspect of creation?

And yet, there it is. Genesis says nothing about this infernal place. Neither does the rest of the Pentateuch (the first five books of the Bible). Neither do the historical books, or the wisdom and poetry books, or the prophets.

What the Old Testament *does* talk about is *sheol*. That is the Hebrew word used 64 times in the Old Testament and translated by Tyndale, and nearly everyone after him, as hell. But *sheol* doesn't mean a dark, fiery, underworld place of torment. It simply means death; the grave; the state of being dead; the "place" of the dead. It has nothing to do with fire, or punishment, or wickedness. It just means death. But look what happens when we anachronistically and unavoidably overlay our popular understanding of hell onto the Hebrew *sheol*. We'll use the King James Version, just for the…well, you know.

- Psalm 9.17: "The wicked shall be turned into **hell**, and all the nations that forget God." David wrote *sheol*, death; we read hell, fiery torment.

- Proverbs 17.27: "Her [the harlot's] house is the way to **hell**, going down to the chambers of death." Solomon wrote *sheol*, the state of death; we read hell, everlasting unbearable fire.

- Isaiah 5.14: "Therefore **hell** hath enlarged herself, and opened her mouth without measure: and their glory, and their multitude, and their pomp, and he that rejoiceth, shall descend into it." Isaiah wrote *sheol*, the realm of the grave; we read hell, the place of unending agony.

When the Old Testament writers use *sheol*, they have no concept of fiery torture, eternal torment, or teeth-grinding outer darkness. They simply mean death. The later Old Testament prophets use the word as a term for "biting the dust" - unraveling, falling apart, collapsing: "I made the nations to shake at the sound of his fall, when I cast him down to **hell** with them that descend into the pit." (Ezekiel 31.16)

By way of review: what does the Old Testament teach us about that dark, fiery, place of torment called hell? Nothing at all.

The New Testament

With the New Testament there is a language change from Hebrew to Greek, and this brings with it another bag of interpretive problems to sort through.

Tyndale and those who later followed in his footsteps translated the Hebrew word *sheol* as hell. But they also used hell as a catch-all word for three *very different* Greek words. And to complicate matters even further, each of these words carries with it definitions, shadings, nuances, and images from the Greek religions from which they originated.

But what's an apostle supposed to do? Matthew, for example. If he is writing the story of Jesus for Greek speaking readers, and if Jesus sits on a hillside somewhere and uses the Hebrew/Aramaic word *sheol*, what is Matthew to do? He has no choice but to borrow a word from their own Greek culture and religion (just like our missionary to the Vikings borrowed their word *hel*), a word that more or less equates to *sheol*, that more or less means the realm or state of death. So Matthew reached down and picks up the word *hades*. He had to. He had no other option. But, boy oh boy, does that make things even more complicated!

Hades

Just like *Hel* is the name of a Norse god and the place she controls, in Greek mythology *Hades* is the name of the god of the underworld, and the place he controls. *Hades* is also known as "the unseen one," because he lived in the underworld so no one ever saw him. He was almost never depicted in Greek art, but - wait for it - when he was painted he was often shown carrying a pitchfork!

In the early development of Greek mythology and religion, *hades* was simply the realm of the dead, the place of death, similar to *sheol* among the Jews. But as the Greek religion developed, *hades* also developed into a place divided in two: one section for the wicked, another for the good.

The "bad place" was called *tartarus*. It was even lower than the underworld and a place of utter captivity. The "good place" had four different levels, but mind you, all still part of *hades*.

- *The Asphodel Meadows*, for ordinary souls, neither really bad nor really good.

- *The Mourning Fields*, for the souls of unrequited lovers and wasted lives.

- *Elysium*, the first level of an actual good place, for those especially righteous souls, where they lived a life of ease and no labor.

- *The Isle of the Blessed*, the island in Elysium was even better than Elysium itself; the ultimate good place.

What must be reiterated, however, is that all of these places, from *Tartarus* to the *Isle of the Blessed* and everything in between, is part of Hades. So, while an Aramaic speaking Jew in first century Judea heard Jesus refer to *sheol*, or as Matthew translated it, *hades*, she would automatically think of the Old Testament idea of a simple place of the dead. But when a person in say, Macedonia, read the word *hades* in Matthew's gospel, he would conjure up Lord knows what from his religious/mythological background.

"And thou, Capernaum, which art exalted unto heaven, shalt be brought down to **hell** [*hades*]." (Matthew 11.23) Down to the grave; down to destruction; down to dust. But how does the Greek reader understand it, or the Norse reader? Or the English reader? Or for that matter, the 21st century Christian reader?

Oy vey! The problems with interpretation! Jews, and Greeks, and Vikings, oh my!

Tartarus

Another word, translated hell in most English Bibles is *tartarus*. You may remember that in Greek mythology it is the lowest of the low places, an inescapable prison of chains and bars located below *Hades* itself. This word is use only once in the entire New Testament, in 2 Peter 2.4: "For if God did not spare angels when they sinned, but cast them into **hell** [*tartarus*] and committed them to chains of gloomy darkness to be kept until the judgment…"

Gehenna

We now come to the third and final Greek word translated into English as hell. And, unlike the first two (*hades* and *tartarus*) which are borrowed from Greek mythology, this word has nothing to do with the underworld. It is actually the name of a valley outside Jerusalem: *Gehenna*, or, the *Valley of Hinnom*.

Gehenna already has a very significant Jewish history before Jesus uses the term. It was the spot where the people of Israel forsook Yahweh, worshiped the god Molech, and offered their children as burnt offerings to this Canaanite deity.

2nd Chronicles describes what happened there under the reign of King Ahaz:

> "Ahaz was twenty years old when he began to reign, and he reigned sixteen years in Jerusalem. And he did not do what was right in the eyes of the Lord, as his father David had done, but he walked in the ways of the kings of Israel. He even made metal images for the Baals, and he made offerings in

> the **Valley of the Son of Hinnom** and burned his sons as an offering, according to the abominations of the nations whom the Lord drove out before the people of Israel. (2 Chronicles 28.1-3).

Ahaz was a wicked and apostate king who worshiped a false god and sacrificed humans, but his son Hezekiah is noted as one of the most righteous kings of all Jewish history. He tore down the Canaanite altars and led a reform, bringing people back to the worship of Yahweh. Then, his son Manasseh, perhaps the most evil king in Jewish history, reversed the accomplishments of his father and followed in the steps of Grandpa Ahaz.

> "Manasseh was twelve years old when he began to reign, and he reigned fifty-five years in Jerusalem. And he did what was evil in the sight of the Lord, according to the abominations of the nations whom the Lord drove out before the

people of Israel. For he rebuilt the high places that his father Hezekiah had broken down, and he erected altars to the Baals, and made Asheroth, and worshiped all the host of heaven and served them…And he burned his sons as an offering in the **Valley of the Son of Hinnom**, and used fortune-telling and omens and sorcery, and dealt with mediums and with necromancers. He did much evil in the sight of the Lord, provoking him to anger." (2 Chronicles 33.1-6)

Mannasseh's grandson Josiah was a righteous king, followed by the wicked king Jehoiakim. It was during Jehoiakim's reign that the prophet Jeremiah prophesied against him and predicted the downfall of Jerusalem and its captivity by Babylon. Give particular attention to the language Jeremiah uses as he described what lay in store for Jerusalem:

"For the sons of Judah have done evil in my sight, declares the Lord. They have set their detestable things in the house that is called by my name, to defile it. And they have built the high places of **Topheth**, which is in the **Valley of the Son of Hinnom**, to burn their sons and their daughters in the fire, which I did not command, nor did it come into my mind. Therefore, behold, the days are coming, declares the Lord, when it will **no more be called Topheth**, or **the Valley of the Son of Hinnom**, but **the Valley of Slaughter**; for **they will bury in Topheth, because there is no room elsewhere**. And the **dead bodies** of this people will be **food for the birds of the air**, and for the beasts of the earth, and none will frighten them away. And I will silence in the cities of Judah and in the streets of Jerusalem the voice of mirth and the voice of gladness, the voice of the bridegroom and the voice of the bride, for **the land shall become a waste.**" (Jeremiah 7.30-34)

Jeremiah is the beginning of the next step in the evolution of the word *Gehenna*. It now moves beyond just being the name of a despicable place, and becomes a prophetic place of destruction, "the Valley of Slaughter." Jeremiah used it to describe the aftermath of Babylonian invasion. Compare this with the language Jesus used 700 years later when he described the looming destruction of Jerusalem by the Roman armies: "Wherever the corpse is, there the vultures will gather." (Matthew 24.28)

Later in his prophecies, Jeremiah reiterates the horrors of the approaching desolation at the hands of the Babylonians:

> "Therefore, behold, days are coming, declares the Lord, when this place shall no more be called **Topheth**, or **the Valley of the Son of Hinnom**, but **the Valley of**

Slaughter. And in this place I will make void the plans of Judah and Jerusalem, and will cause their people to fall by the sword before their enemies, and by the hand of those who seek their life. I will give their dead bodies for food to the birds of the air and to the beasts of the earth. And **I will make this city a horror**, a thing to be hissed at. Everyone who passes by it will be horrified and will hiss because of all its wounds. And I will make them eat the flesh of their sons and their daughters, and everyone shall eat the flesh of his neighbor in the siege and in the distress, with which their enemies and those who seek their life afflict them…Men shall **bury in Topheth because there will be no place else to bury**. Thus will I do to this place, declares the Lord, and to its inhabitants, **making this city like Topheth**. The houses of Jerusalem and the houses of the kings of Judah —all the houses on whose roofs offerings have been offered to all the host of heaven, and drink offerings have been poured out to other gods—shall be **defiled like the place of Topheth**.'" (Jeremiah 19.6-13)

And this is the last mention of *Gehenna/Topheth* in the Old Testament. The word *Gehenna* transitioned from being just the name of an actual accursed valley outside Jerusalem, a place of human sacrifices, into now being the term for the utter destruction that awaited the entire city at the hands of its foreign enemy. As for the place itself, it remained off limits, considered cursed; no one built homes there or planted vineyards. Much later, in the 13th century, Jewish rabbis taught that the valley actually became the city dump. That may be the case, but there is no ancient source documenting it. Nevertheless, by the time of Jesus *Gehenna* had become a term describing, not the place of an afterlife of unending punishment, but the end result of Jerusalem turning to evil and aligning itself with worldly powers rather than with God. Those worldly powers, in the end, turn on Jerusalem and devour it. Jeremiah warned of Babylon, Jesus warned of Rome.

There you have it. One Hebrew word (*sheol*), two Greek words (*hades* and *tartarus*), and one proper name (*Gehenna*), and they all get translated into English with the single word hell, automatically conjuring in the mind of the modern reader images derived more from medieval poetry and art than from Scripture itself.

Chapter Five

The Apostles

We have looked at the various words used in Scripture which get translated as hell, and we have seen that when hell is defined as a place of unending torment the Old Testament says nothing at all about it. Now let's turn our attention to what the New Testament teaches us about hell. We will begin with the Apostles and then work our way back to Jesus himself.

The Book of Acts

In the book of Acts we find the earliest examples of Christian theology, that is, the apostolic sermons recorded by Luke. Depending on how you count them, there are a dozen or more sermons, some to Jews, some to Greeks, some to Roman dignitaries, some to Christians. There are sermons by Stephen, Peter, James, and Paul.

A good many of these sermons are evangelistic. Now, in the tradition in which I grew up, Sunday nights were considered the "evangelistic services," and we invited our friends to come hear the preaching and perhaps give their lives to Christ. In its most basic structure, the Sunday night sermon went something like this: (1) God created the world good, (2) humans sinned and made it bad, (3) we are all sinners headed to hell, (4) Jesus offers heaven instead. In headline form, when we were witnessing to the lost, the message of those sermons became something like, "If you were to die tonight, do you know where you would spend eternity?" Evangelistic sermons. Doing evangelism. So, surely the original evangelists, the Apostles, said something similar, right? I mean, after all, they are the ones from whom we take our cues.

Here is the problem: in all the sermons recorded in the book of Acts, not a single one of them says anything whatsoever about hell! The evangelistic message of the Apostles wasn't, "Accept Jesus as your personal Lord and Savior so you too can avoid the everlasting tormenting fires of hell." Instead, the apostolic proclamation was, "Jesus Christ is risen from the dead and he is Lord. Repent and be baptized into Christ who is victorious over sin and death!" But mention hell? Not. One. Single. Time.

Saint Paul

Ok. So, Luke, Stephen, Peter, James, John and Paul have nothing to say about hell in the book of Acts. But when we arrive at Paul's epistles, in which he develops and expands and defines his doctrines and theology, surely we will find his insights into the subject of everlasting torment. Somewhere, maybe in his *magnus opus*, the Epistle to the Romans, or in his decidedly eschatological First Epistle to the Corinthians, he will give us the inside scoop on the apostolic doctrine of hell.

Again: Not. One. Single. Time. Not in his major letters, his prison letters, his pastoral epistles - nowhere in his writings does Paul refer to hell as an everlasting destination for the wicked or for unbelievers.

The Other Epistles

It comes as a surprise to us that Paul doesn't teach us anything about hell. He teaches us about Jesus, about sin, baptism, communion, church life, the gifts of the spirit, walking in Christ, being filled with the Spirit, the hope of resurrection, and a host of other things, but nary a mention of hell. Maybe it was an oversight on his part, since the doctrine of eternal torment is such an important one.

Perhaps New Testament teaching about hell is left to James, Jude, John, and the writer of Hebrews. Except, the thing is, none of their epistles say anything about hell either!

Peter does say something about *tartarus*, in 1 Peter 3.18-20: "For Christ also suffered once for sins, the righteous for the unrighteous, that he might bring us to God, being put to death in the flesh but made alive in the spirit, *in which he went and* *proclaimed to the spirits in **prison** [tartarus]*, because they formerly did not obey, when God's patience waited in the days of Noah, while the ark was being prepared, in which a few, that is, eight persons, were brought safely through water." But the point of Peter's words isn't a warning about being burned alive for eternity, rather a proclamation that Christ so destroyed the power of death that he descended to the lowest of the low places, to the very depths of death itself, and there preached to the prisoners in that place. And what, do you suppose, Jesus preached? I would suggest he preached what he always did: the coming of the Kingdom of God. He preached the Good News.

How could all of these apostolic writers overlook this issue of utmost importance? Didn't they know that Jesus himself talks about hell (more about this in the next chapter)? How could they ignore it if Jesus taught about it? Unless, maybe, they understood what Jesus said about the subject in a way significantly different than the way later generations would understand it. Is it possible that these original followers of Jesus - these men taught, trained and sent out by the Lord himself - knew that Jesus wasn't threatening everlasting torture, so they didn't either?

The Book of Revelation

We come now to the last book of the New Testament, The Revelation of Jesus Christ. It is an apocalyptic book. Part of it deals with judgment day and the new creation. It talks about heaven. And it tells us three things about hell. Well, about *hades*.

- It tells us that Christ has the keys to *hades*: "I died, and behold I am alive forevermore, and I have the keys of Death and **Hades**." (1.18)

- It tells us that in the end, *hades* gives up the dead: "Death and **Hades** gave up the dead who were in them, and they were judged, each one of them, according to what they had done." (20.13)

- And finally, in the very next verse, it tells us that *hades* itself, the realm of death, is destined to be cast into the lake of fire: "Then Death and **Hades** were thrown into the lake of fire. This is the second death, the lake of fire." (20.14)

Wait just a minute! If Luke, Paul, Peter, James, John, and Jude teach us nothing about hell, and don't even mention it, then from just exactly where do we get teaching about hell?

I thought you'd never ask. We get it from Jesus.

Chapter Six

What Jesus Said About Hell

It may have come as quite a shock that neither the Old Testament nor the apostolic epistles say anything about a hell of everlasting anguish and tormenting fire. One might assume, from all the real estate it has taken up in preaching and evangelism, that it would be found from start to finish in the Scriptures. But clearly, it wasn't on the radar of the Old Testament people of God, and it wasn't significant enough for *any* of the apostles to write about it in their epistles, not even once. From whence, then, do we get any biblical information about hell? Well, from the original source. From the lips of Jesus. From the teachings of God in the flesh.

Jesus And Gehenna

Before we delve into his words, keep in mind two things. First, Jesus probably isn't saying the things about hell that we've been told he's saying, and second, in every single case listed below, Jesus uses the word *Gehenna*. Remember *Gehenna*? The place of apostasy and human sacrifice, the place Jeremiah called "The Valley of Slaughter," the place that became a byword for the devastation Babylon was about to bring down on Jerusalem, the place where bodies would be piled and birds of the air would feast on them - that is the word Jesus uses in all these instances.

There are four different instances when Jesus talks about "hell" - well, what has been translated hell in English Bibles. Let me start over. There are four different instances when Jesus talks about the valley of Gehenna. The actual word is used a total of 12 times in the New Testament, 11 from the lips of Jesus, and one from the pen of his brother James (who writes that the tongue is a small but dangerous instrument set on fire by hell; James 3.6). Of the 11 cases of Jesus using the word, four of them are duplicates. So, contrary to the popular line that, "Jesus spoke more about hell than he did about heaven" (which is utter nonsense), Jesus used the word seven times in three different settings. Let's look at them.

The first time we see *Gehenna* used in the New Testament it is when Jesus is delivering the Sermon on the Mount in Matthew 5. He warns about anger, insults and imprecations in verse 22: "But I say to you that everyone who is angry with his brother will be liable to judgment; whoever insults his brother will be liable to the council; and whoever says, 'You fool!' will be liable to the hell [*gehenna*] of fire."

Just to be clear, we should pay careful attention to the first century Jewish context of these words. "Judgment" is a reference to the lowest court in the land - the local tribunal. "The council" is literally "the Sanhedrin [Gr.: *synedrion*]," the supreme court in Jerusalem. And finally, "the hell of fire" is the fire of Gehenna [Gr.: *gehenna tou pyr*].

In the Sermon on the Mount Jesus is unfolding the ethics for living in the Kingdom of God. People might observe the law by not murdering, but still carry murder in their hearts. Jesus is calling for something deeper than actions without attitudes. He is calling for a transformation of our inner being. It isn't enough that people don't murder; the ethics of the Kingdom of God call for them to lay aside malice, evil speaking, and slander. Jesus is offering a better way of life, but if that way is rejected, the downward progression will be first getting into a mess on the local level, then it becoming a matter for the supreme council, but ultimately, Gehenna; ultimately finding yourself in a place of destruction, a place of anguish, a place of accursedness, a hell of a place.

Is Jesus speaking of a condition in this life, or in the life hereafter? I believe the answer is yes. Surely you know people whose lives in the here and now are a living hell because of the hatred and unforgiveness they have held in their hearts. They are already "in hell," and that follows them into the next life, if and until they are changed. This is as true for 21st century people as it was for the original audience in the first century.

A few verses later, in the same chapter and in the same "sermon," Jesus uses the word again: "If your right eye causes you to sin, tear it out and throw it away. For it is better that you lose one of your members than that your whole body be thrown into hell [*gehenna*]. And if your right hand causes you to sin, cut it off and throw it away. For it is better that you lose one of your members than that your whole body go into hell [*gehenna*]." (Matthew 5.29-30; Jesus says this exact thing again in Matthew 18.9.)

There is a story that the early church theologian Origen took these and other verses literally and castrated himself (not likely a true story, seeing that Origen wasn't given to literal interpretations of Scripture, and the tale is handed down by someone who greatly disliked him). This supposed bad action left a dark stain on Origen's reputation throughout the rest of history. Why on earth would he do such a thing? Didn't he know Jesus wasn't being literal? I bet you have never met a pastor, a Christian counselor, or anyone else who has seriously suggested someone gouge out their eye because they couldn't help staring at women. You've never met a Christian who would counsel a petty thief to cut off her hand because it would keep her from shoplifting. Dig into all the different commentaries on this text and you will find that none of them suggest Jesus meant this literally. He was speaking metaphorically. He was saying, "take decisive action to avoid temptation." Why, then, when we get to that one little word twice used here, do people insist Jesus is referring to a literal postmortem place of everlasting torment? Again, he is saying giving in to temptation instead of thwarting it, cutting it off at the bud, ends up with your life (both here and hereafter) being in a place of utter ruin.

The next occasion Jesus speaks of *Gehenna* is in Matthew 10, where he commissions the twelve disciples and instructs them to take the Gospel throughout Judea. He tells them things like, "Don't go to the Gentiles, stick with the Jews," and, "Shake the dust from your feet if they reject you," and, "You're going to get persecuted, hated." This, by the way, wasn't a general truth for all Christians in all times; it was specifically for the mission of the Twelve to the people of Judah. In that context, Jesus said, "And do not fear those who kill the body but cannot kill the soul. Rather fear him who can destroy both soul and body in hell [*gehenna*]." (Matthew 10.28).

The context of this saying is Jesus telling his Twelve to not be afraid, even though they faced persecution and death. Then he warns them in this verse that there is someone they should be afraid of (some interpreters and commentators have argued this someone is God, while others have argued it is Satan and his demonic forces against which Christians battle). And then, in the following verses, Jesus again tells the disciples to be not afraid. But, whatever he is saying, I would suggest, he is not threatening his disciples with eternity in tormenting flames. As he so often does, N.T. Wright sheds light on the verse with his comments:

> Jesus believed that Israel was faced in his day by enemies at two quite different levels. There were the obvious

ones: Rome, Herod, and their underlings. They were the ones who had the power to kill the body. But there were other, darker enemies, who had the power to kill the **soul** as well: enemies who were battling for that soul even now, during Jesus' ministry, and who were using the more obvious enemies as a cover. Actually, it's even worse than that. The demonic powers that are greedy for the soul of God's people are using their very desire for justice and vengeance as the bait on the hook. The people of light are never more at risk than when they are lured into fighting the darkness with more darkness. That is the road straight to the smouldering rubbish-tip, to Gehenna, and Jesus wants his followers to be well aware of it. This is what you should be afraid of. [3]

---

[3] Wright, T. (2004). *Matthew for Everyone, Part 1: Chapters 1-15* (p. 119). London: Society for Promoting Christian Knowledge.

The third setting in which we find Jesus speaking of Gehenna is when he rebukes the religious leaders of his day in Matthew 23. In verse 15 he says, "Woe to you, scribes and Pharisees, hypocrites! For you travel across sea and land to make a single proselyte, and when he becomes a proselyte, you make him twice as much a child of hell [*gehenna*] as yourselves."

Which do you think Jesus is most likely saying here: a child of hell, as in a child of unimaginably painful unending torture that comes after death, or a child of *Gehenna* as in, coming to the end of the line and it being a very bad condition, a wasted life, a life not built on the things of God, a life that is more of a curse than a blessing, a life that is ruined and void of God's favor, not because he withheld it, but because the person refused it?

In this same speech, Jesus said, "You serpents, you brood of vipers, how are you to escape being sentenced to hell [*gehenna*]?" (v. 33)

Let us look at this verse (and the one previously mentioned) in its broader context. Matthew 23 (from which this verse is taken) contains the "Woes" that Jesus speaks over the Jewish religious leaders of the time ("Woe to you, scribes, Pharisees, hypocrites…"). The very next chapter is Jesus' vivid description of the soon to come ("this generation shall not pass away until all these things take place," v. 34) destruction of Jerusalem by the Roman armies - a destruction he foresaw, forewarned, and wept over. But now, read the verses surrounding this "brood of vipers, how are you to escape being sentenced to *gehenna*" line:

> "Woe to you, scribes and Pharisees, hypocrites! For you build the tombs of the prophets and decorate the monuments of the righteous, saying, 'If we had lived in the days of our fathers, we would not have taken part with them in shedding the blood of the

prophets.' Thus you witness against yourselves that you are sons of those who murdered the prophets. Fill up, then, the measure of your fathers. You serpents, you brood of vipers, **how are you to escape being sentenced to hell** [*gehenna*]? Therefore I send you prophets and wise men and scribes, some of whom you will kill and crucify, and some you will flog in your synagogues and persecute from town to town, so that on you may come all the righteous blood shed on earth, from the blood of righteous Abel to the blood of Zechariah the son of Barachiah, whom you murdered between the sanctuary and the altar. **Truly, I say to you, all these things will come upon this generation.** O Jerusalem, Jerusalem, the city that kills the prophets and stones those who are sent to it! How often would I have gathered your children together as a hen gathers her brood under her wings, and you were not willing! See, your house is left to you desolate." (Matthew 23.29-38)

As Jerusalem faces imminent destruction from Rome, Jesus is taking on the same role that Jeremiah did 700 years before when Jerusalem faced imminent destruction from Babylon. He even uses the same imagery, the same language, the same word: *gehenna*. I find it interesting that what he warns the Apostles to be aware of (persecution, rejection, death) in chapter 10 is precisely the same - even in the words used - as he accuses the religious leaders of enacting in chapter 23. And in both contexts he uses the word *gehenna* to describe the hell of it all.[4]

In all of these texts, the backdrop is the approaching destruction of Jerusalem by the Roman armies. This looming destruction, like the Babylonian invasion before it, stands as a kind of symbol of the

---

[4] The other Gospel uses of *gehenna* are parallels to the instances in Matthew. Cf. Mark 9.43-47, Luke 12.5).

consequences of living a life rejecting God and his ways, but in none of these texts is Jesus describing a literal underworld place of unending torment designed by God as the eternal destination of most of humanity.

And this is why the Apostles didn't say anything about it in their letters.

Jesus And Hades

Everyone knows that Jesus was a storyteller. In fact, about a third of his recorded teachings are in the form of stories and parables: the Prodigal Son, the Sower and the Seeds, the Good Samaritan and dozens more. But what a lot of people aren't aware of is that many of these stories were not original with Jesus. Teaching in parables was the stock trade of rabbis in Jesus' time, and some stories were told by one teacher, heard, maybe written down, reworked a bit by the next teacher, retold to a different group, and passed along to other rabbis, not unlike how sermon illustrations make the rounds in modern times.

One of the tales that Jesus borrowed from someone else, tweaked a little, and retold for his own purpose is the parable of the Rich Man and Lazarus in Luke 16. Take a minute and reread it, and then let's talk about how and why Jesus changed it up and made it his own.

> "There was a rich man who was clothed in purple and fine linen and who feasted sumptuously every day. And at his gate was laid a poor man named Lazarus, covered with sores, who desired to be fed with what fell from the rich man's table. Moreover, even the dogs came and licked his sores. The poor man died and was carried by the angels to Abraham's side. The rich man also died and was buried, and in **Hades**, being in torment, he lifted up his eyes and saw Abraham far off and Lazarus at his side. And he called out, 'Father Abraham, have mercy

on me, and send Lazarus to dip the end of his finger in water and cool my tongue, for I am in anguish in this flame.' But Abraham said, 'Child, remember that you in your lifetime received your good things, and Lazarus in like manner bad things; but now he is comforted here, and you are in anguish. And besides all this, between us and you a great chasm has been fixed, in order that those who would pass from here to you may not be able, and none may cross from there to us.' And he said, 'Then I beg you, father, to send him to my father's house - for I have five brothers - so that he may warn them, lest they also come into this place of torment.' But Abraham said, 'They have Moses and the Prophets; let them hear them.' And he said, 'No, father Abraham, but if someone goes to them from the dead, they will repent.' He said to him, 'If they do not hear Moses and the Prophets, neither will they be convinced if someone should rise from the dead.'" (Luke 16.19-31)

Many assume the whole point of this parable is to teach something about hell. I want to suggest that is not the purpose of this story at all. Take a look at what Jesus is talking about throughout this chapter in Luke:

- "There was a **rich man**…" (v. 1)

- "The Pharisees, who were **lovers of money**, heard all these things, and they ridiculed him… (v. 14)

- "There was a **rich man** who was clothed in purple and fine linen and who feasted sumptuously every day. (v. 19)

You tell me, what was Jesus focusing on here? Now, let's unpack the story a bit and pay attention to the little additions Jesus made to the original version.

"Clothed in purple and fine linen…" Jesus isn't talking about just any rich man;

this is the attire of a high priest (cf. Exodus 39.27-39).

"Send him to my father's house - for I have five brothers…" Annas, the high priest when Jesus was born, was appointed to that powerful position by the Roman government. He was deposed ten years later (in the year A.D. 15), but remained one of the most politically powerful figures in Jerusalem throughout the life of Jesus. Although deposed, he still carried the title and rank of high priest and ruled from behind the scenes through his son in law, the high priest Caiaphas and…watch this… through his **five sons**, all of whom served as high priests (Interestingly, one of the sons was named Theophilus. He served as high priest from 37 to 41, and some believe him to be the Theophilus for whom Luke and Acts were written).

Just to be clear. There was a rich man named Annas, backed by Rome, who ruled as high priest. He had five sons who were also high priests, as well as a son in law. Is it just coincidence that Jesus modifies this stock tale with the information about the vesture and family size of this man who finds himself in Hades?

But, there is more! Jesus tells us that the poor man in the story was, "**named Lazarus**." Lazarus, that is, Eleazar, was not a unique name in Jerusalem, in fact one of the five sons of Annas had that name. But, one has to wonder if Jesus intentionally named the character in this story after one of his closest friends, Lazarus of Bethany, himself from Jerusalem aristocracy and known among the high priest's family. And is it just coincidence that the story has the very rich but very dead high priest asking that Lazarus be sent back to the land of the living to warn the five brothers about living an uncaring and selfish life? And when Jesus has Abraham saying, "If they do not hear Moses and the Prophets, neither will they be convinced if someone should **rise from the dead**," is he referring to his friend Lazarus' rising? Oh, and one more thing: isn't it a startling additional piece of the puzzle to learn that this precise family would not believe Jesus even "if someone should rise from the dead," and instead plotted to have Lazarus killed because so many were following Jesus as a result of his rising from the dead (John 12.10)?

In any case, this fascinating reshaping of an already taught story isn't a lesson on the details of a literal hell. It is an ever so slightly veiled rebuke of the most corrupt and powerful family in Jerusalem, and a warning to everyone that living a life of selfishness and not caring for the poor doesn't put you in the Kingdom of God, no matter how religious you are, but brings you down to the depths of Hades instead. This is, by the way, the very thing Jesus teaches us we will all be judged for on judgment day.

Chapter Seven

Eternal Fire

Just because Jesus didn't speak of a literal, everlasting, unrelenting, tormenting, hellfire doesn't mean he didn't talk about a fire of judgment. He did, and so did St. Paul. They both also weigh in on what judgment day will be like for all of us.

Jesus speaks of a judgment of fire in three different places:

- Mt. 18.8: "And if your hand or your foot causes you to sin, cut it off and throw it away. It is better for you to enter life crippled or lame than with two hands or two feet to be thrown into the **eternal fire**."

- Mt. 25.41: "Then he will say to those on his left, 'Depart from me, you cursed, into the **eternal fire** prepared for the devil and his angels.'"

- Mark 9.49: "For everyone will be salted with **fire**."

Isn't Forever Long Enough?

Have you ever wondered why we use the phrase, even in the Our Father or Lord's Prayer, "forever and ever"? Is that second ever even necessary? Is there anything longer than forever? That second ever is a relic of translation. It is what scientists call a vestigial remnant, an unnecessary leftover of something that was there before. Some snakes, for example, have vestigial remnant pelvis bones. Go figure.

Stumbling upon this phrase, "forever and ever," is the linguistic equivalent of going on an archeological dig in some east coast Native American village, and discovering 11th century Viking jewelry. When we see it, we are surprised it is there, and we wonder where it came from, and we know there must be a story to be explored. It is evidence of something unexpected in the past.

The Greek word translated "Forever and ever" is *aionios*. The problem is, *aionios* is plural. But, it isn't the plural of "forever," as if there could be two, or ten, or forty seven forevers. It is the plural of *aion*, from which we get the word eon, and which means ages. The

Greek word translated, "forever and ever" literally means, "ages and ages."

Which leads us to another question: just how long *is* an age? Well, it all depends on what we are talking about. Scientists tell us that the Jurassic Age was 56 million years. On the other hand, the Viking Age was about 250 years, and the Middle Ages (note: plural) was 1,000 years. When a dear friend says, "Man, I haven't seen you in ages," she may mean six months, and when my daughter says, "Dad, I had to stand in line for ages at the store today," she might mean 20 minutes.

So, how long is an age? There is no telling. An age isn't a specific amount of time, but it is a specific segment of time. An age, an eon, an *aion*, is a **definite period of time with a beginning *and an end*.** Let me say that last part again because it is integral to the discussion at hand: ***and an end***. So, *aionios*, translated "forever and ever," literally means, "for ages and ages."

Aionios gets translated "forever and ever" because the word is trying to communicate an idea that transcends time. It is not a word about duration, but about the quality, the nature, the source of a thing. Think of *aionios* like this: going *beyond* this age.

In the Apostles Creed we confess that we believe in "the life everlasting (*zoen aionion*)." In 325 that creed was expanded into what we call the Nicene Creed, and that was expanded even more at the Council of Constantinople in 381 when the section regarding the Holy Spirit was added. That council was presided over by St. Gregory of Nyssa, "the Father of Fathers" (who, by the way believed in the future restoration of all creation, including all people), and he tweaked the Apostles Creeds' "life everlasting (*zoen aionion*)" to "life of the world to come (*zoen tou mellontos aionos*)." The Greek *mellontos* means "coming" or "to come." Gregory changes it, ever so slightly; it isn't eternal life, with a focus on duration, it is the life "of the age to come," with a focus on the source of the life. What we Christians believe in isn't just living forever, but living a completely new kind of life, a heavenly life, a life with its source in a realm beyond our space-time continuum.

Let me approach this from one more angle and see if this helps. In English we have two related words, eternal and eternity. But we use them very differently. When we say eternal, we are speaking of duration, an unending duration. But when we speak of eternity - "when we step into eternity…" - we are speaking about a different reality, a different realm, a different world, a different state of being. *That* is what *aionios* means; it is more about eternity than eternal.

Before I leave the creeds, as an aside I would like to point out that our ancient confessions of faith do not address the issue of postmortem never ending torment, but they do emphasize the resurrection of the dead, and the life of the age to come.

There is a good chance that by now you have forgotten what we were originally talking about, because, well, it's been ages since we first started this chapter. But, we were talking about "eternal fire," and I've just spent the last five pages explaining that the word translated eternal isn't about time, but source. Perhaps a better translation would be "the fire of eternity," or, "the fire of the ages of ages," or even, "fire of the age to come."

Jesus isn't speaking of a literal fire, he isn't speaking of any kind of fire of this world, and he isn't speaking about a fire that torments and tortures forever. He is speaking of a fire from the heavenly realm, the very fire of God, the purifying, cleansing, restoring, re-creating fire with which *everyone* must be "salted." Some, I would argue, will be salted more than others.

The Fire of Judgment

We're not talking about hell now; not that terrifying underworld place of unending fiery torment. No, we are talking about purifying fire.

Sometimes in this life, hitting rock bottom is what begins a process of restoration. Think of the prodigal son who finds himself eating slop with the pigs and this becomes the turning point for restoration to his father (Luke 15.11-32). Even in this life, God can use the troubles we get ourselves into as an instrument to bring us back to him. People sometimes make a life of hell for themselves, come to a place where they realize this isn't working at all and is only getting worse, and turn their hearts to the One who can save them. Finding yourself in Gehenna can be the beginning of finding your way to heaven.

Moreover, the troubles of this life are often unrelated to sin or bad choices, and sometimes occur even as we serve Christ. St. Peter wrote, "Beloved, do not be surprised at the **fiery trial** when it comes upon you to test you, as though something strange were happening to you." (1 Peter 4.12) Those fiery trials, painful as they are, bring us closer to our Lord.

When the Apostle Paul describes judgment day, he also uses the imagery of fire:

> Now if anyone builds on the foundation with gold, silver, precious stones, wood, hay, straw— each one's work will become manifest, for the Day will disclose it, because it will be revealed **by fire**, and **the fire** will test what sort of work each one has done. If the work that anyone has built on the foundation survives, he will receive a reward. If anyone's work is **burned up**, he will suffer loss, though he himself will be saved, but only as through **fire**. (1 Corinthians 3.12-15)

Each one of us is going to be tested as though by fire. Each one of us must be "salted" with fire. It happens in this life, and in the life to come. When Jesus speaks of "eternal fire," "fire of the age to come," he is not warning about some never ending torture; he is warning about a life lived without reference to the things of God, which ends up, both in this life and the life to come, enflamed. But not the flames of unending torment, rather the flames of cleansing, the flames that burn away every shoddy thing I've done in life, every sinful thought, word, or deed, the flame that burns so the soul may be brought fully into union with God. "Our God is a consuming fire." (Hebrews 12.29)

Chapter Eight

Avoiding The Flames

We've been discussing the various ways Christians have understood hell through the ages. Some see it as a place of unending torment, some as a fire that completely annihilates, and some as a place or process where everything that holds us back from union with God is burned away. Robert Capon refers to the cleansing fire as, "the white hot fury of the love of God." St. Isaac the Syrian wrote, "Those who are punished in Gehenna are scourged by the scourge of love...For the sorrow caused in the heart by sin against love is sharper than any torment that can be. It would be improper for a man to think that sinners in Gehenna are deprived of the love of God...Thus I say that this is the torment of Gehenna: bitter regret. But love inebriates the souls of the sons of Heaven by its delectability."[5] The late Catholic theologian Peter Kreeft wrote, "The very fires of Hell are made of the love of God!"[6]

When we talk about the fire "from the age to come" we are really talking about part of the process of salvation itself. In much of the American church, particularly those parts strongly influenced by the doctrine of

---

[5] St. Isaac of Ninevah, *The Ascetical Homilies of St Isaac the Syrian*, Homily 72: On the Vision of the Nature of Incorporeal Beings; Holy Transfiguration Monastery, Boston, 2011.

[6] Kreeft, Peter, *Everything You Ever Wanted To Know About Heaven*, p. 235, Ignatius Press, San Francisco, 1990.

penal substitutionary atonement[7], salvation is about being moved from the guilty column to the not guilty column because Jesus paid for our sins. This view teaches that in a heavenly legal move, God poured out his wrath on the Son so he wouldn't have to pour it out on us, and now he looks at us as guiltless, although we really aren't. It is a kind of heavenly legal fiction happening here.

But this will not do. Salvation is not a legal game, it is being truly transformed into the image of Jesus Christ himself, reflecting him, being like him, being changed by him, being made one with him. St. Paul writes that we are to, "be transformed by the renewal of your minds," and, "be conformed to the image of his Son." (Romans 12.2, 8.29)

In the age to come the fire of the heavenly realm is going to refine us and

---

[7] See my book, *Salvation And How We Got It Wrong*, Mayeux Press, Denison, TX, 2013

burn away everything that keeps us from being conformed to the image of Christ. However, we can ameliorate that experience by becoming more like Jesus in the here and now. The spiritual transformation we must experience is not reserved for the afterlife. Paul writes that we, "*are* being transformed into the same image from one degree of glory to another." (2 Corinthians 3.18) It is present tense, an ongoing process.

Everyone of us will stand before God and be judged. By judged, I do not mean condemned, rather, we will be made the way we ought to be. And *that* will involve the salting, the testing, the purging, the fire. For some the fire will be more intense than for others. But, there are things we can do in *this* life to lessen the intensity of that day. Let me say it in a straightforward and clear way: We can lessen the purging fire by *being like Jesus in this life*.

Judgment Day

Some Christians misguidedly believe that our salvation has nothing to do with our works, only our faith. But real faith, true belief, isn't simply mental assent. True faith (*pistis*) includes allegiance to Christ and his ways, and true allegiance impacts what we *do*. It affects how we live our lives.

In fact, every time the Bible describes judgment day, it tells us that we are really judged for our works (including our thoughts, words, and deeds), and particularly for how we treat one another.

Please take the time to carefully read what Jesus and the Apostles tell us about judgment day:

- Matthew 16.27: "For the Son of Man is going to come with his angels in the glory of his Father, and then he will repay each person according to **what he has done**."

- Matthew 25: 34-40: "Then the King will say to those on his right, "'Come, you who are blessed by my Father, inherit the kingdom prepared for you from the foundation of the world. For I was hungry and you gave me food, I was thirsty and you gave me drink, I was a stranger and you welcomed me, I was naked and you clothed me, I was sick and you visited me, I was in prison and you came to me.' Then the righteous will answer him, saying, 'Lord, when did we see you hungry and feed you, or thirsty and give you drink? And when did we see you a stranger and welcome you, or naked and clothe you? And when did we see you sick or in prison and visit you?' And the King will answer them, 'Truly, I say to you, *as you **did** it to one of the least of these my brothers, you **did** it to me*.'"

- 1 Corinthians 3.10-15: According to the grace of God given to me, like a skilled master builder I laid a foundation, and someone else is building upon it. Let each one take care how he builds upon it. For no one can lay a foundation other than that which is laid, which is Jesus Christ. Now if anyone builds on the foundation with gold, silver, precious stones, wood, hay, straw - **each one's work** will become manifest, for the Day will disclose it, because it will be revealed by fire, and the fire will test what sort of work each one has done. If **the work** that anyone has built on the foundation survives, he will receive a reward. If anyone's **work** is burned up, he will suffer loss, though he himself will be saved, but only as through fire.

- 2 Corinthians 5.10: For we must all appear before the judgment seat of Christ, so that each one may receive what is due for **what he has done** in the body, whether good or evil.

- Revelation 20.11-13: Then I saw a great white throne and him who was seated on it. From his presence earth and sky fled away, and no place was found for them. And I saw the dead, great and small, standing before the throne, and books were opened. Then another book was opened, which is the book of life. And the dead were judged by what was written in the books, **according to what they had done**. And the sea gave up the dead who were in it, Death and Hades gave up the dead who were in them, and they were judged, each one of them, **according to what they had done**.

- Revelation 22.12: "Behold, I am coming soon, bringing my recompense with me, to repay everyone for **what he has done**."

What we do matters. It matters a lot. It matters in this life, and it will matter when we stand before God in the life to come. True Christian faith isn't merely assenting to a group of doctrines or believing something about Jesus. And there is no such thing as "faith alone." The only time "faith alone" is found in the Bible it is from the pen of James, the brother of our Lord. Combatting the notion that faith is just some kind of intellectual assent or spiritual exercise that doesn't really affect what we do and how we live, James wrote, "What good is it, my brothers, if someone says he has faith but does not have **works**? Can that faith save him? If a brother or sister is poorly clothed and lacking in daily food, and one of you says to them, 'Go in peace, be warmed and filled,' without giving them the things needed for the body, what good is that? So also faith by itself, if it does not have **works**, is dead…You see that a person is **justified by works** and not by **faith alone**." (James 2.14-17, 24)

True Christian faith is expressed in a life spent doing what Jesus did; being like our Lord.

Doing Good

There is a striking sentence about Jesus in one of Peter's sermons in Acts: "He went about **doing good** and healing all who were oppressed by the devil, for God was with him." (Acts 10.38) Doing good and setting people free from the devilish works that have entangled them is what the Christian life is all about. We imitate Jesus by doing good. If we truly understand the depth of his love for us, we will have no choice: we will be compelled to love in action.

The O.T. prophet Micah summarized our entire spiritual walk with these words, "He has shown you oh man what is good, and what does the Lord require of you, but do justly, to love mercy, and to walk humbly with your God." (Micah 6.8) Just those three things: do justice, love mercy, walk in humility before God.

Jesus made it even more simple:

> But when the Pharisees heard that he had silenced the Sadducees, they gathered together. And one of them, a lawyer, asked him a question to test him. "Teacher, which is the great commandment in the Law?" And he said to him, "You shall love the Lord your God with all your heart and with all your soul and with all your mind. This is the great and first commandment. And a second is like it: You shall love your neighbor as yourself. On these two commandments depend all the Law and the Prophets." (Matthew 22.34-40)

Moses gives us ten things, Micah gives us three, and Jesus narrows it down to just two: love God, and love your neighbor.

Do you want to be more like Jesus in this life, and avoid the fire both in this life and life in the age to come? Do this: love God, and love your neighbor. This is what it means to "work out your own salvation," as St. Paul instructs us. And even then it isn't really us doing all the work, "for it is God who works in you, both to will and to work for his good pleasure." (Philippians 2.12-13)

One last thing. Are you familiar with that text in the book of Hebrews which encourages the readers to lay aside the basics and move on to a more mature faith, to move from milk to meat? The basics listed are doctrinal things: "Therefore let us leave the elementary doctrine of Christ…" we are told. But have you ever wondered what we move *toward*? Perhaps there are some deeply spiritual doctrines that babes in Christ can't fathom, or maybe secrets to spiritual gifts and power, or understanding deep mysteries. Ah, but no. Hebrews tells us precisely what it is we are to move on to, precisely what it is that is evidence we are maturing in our faith. The writer speaks about fields bearing good crops and bad crops, and then writes, "in your case, beloved, we feel sure of better things -

things that belong to salvation. For God is not unjust so as to overlook **your work** and **the love that you have shown** for his name in serving the saints, as you still do." (Hebrews 6.1, 9-10)

If God himself were to ask for your help, would you give it? Jesus said, "If you have done it to the least of these my brothers, you have done it to me." There are more needs in this world than you and I can respond to. But we *can* respond to some. I can't change everyone's life, but I can change someone's life. I can't save everyone. But I can save someone. We can give our time, our money, our tears, our muscle-power, our prayers, our selves. And every time we do, we are partnering with God to change the world, and in the process we become more like Jesus. Salvation isn't being moved over from the guilty column to the not guilty column. Salvation is being made like Jesus and brought into union with God. The more we care for and love others, the more God does the work of making us like himself.

If you build with good stuff, the fire doesn't burn it.

Chapter Nine

Jesus Saves

Some Christians believe Jesus died and rose again to save only, "the elect," those people that God has predestined to enjoy eternity with him. Everyone else, the great majority of humanity, he has predestined to eternal damnation.

Other Christians believe that Jesus died and rose again to save everyone, that it is God's will that all be saved, but because fallen and lost humanity has free will which God will not override, even though God wills it, not everyone will be saved, only those who, in their sinful fallenness, freely choose the salvation offered. Most people, however, don't, and the end result is much the same as the first group - the great majority of humanity will be sent to eternal damnation.

The interesting thing is that people from each of these groups of Christians, although they strongly disagree with each other's understanding of how salvation in Christ works, still recognize each other as faithful believers, and as within the pale of acceptable Christian doctrine. "I'm convinced you are wrong, but you aren't a heretic!"

But, a lot of people from each of these groups of Christians consider people from a third group to be beyond the pale. They look at people in this third group as severely misguided to the point of tiptoeing right up to the edge of heresy and most likely hopping over the line. They mischaracterize people in this third group and say they don't understand salvation, don't understand the uniqueness of Christ, and don't see Jesus as the only path to salvation.

And what do Christians in this third group believe that makes them such pariahs? They believe that what Jesus accomplished in his incarnation, death, and resurrection is so powerful, so world changing, so transformative, so magnificent, and so cosmic in its scope, that the result is not that only a small elect number are saved, not that only a minority who exercised their free will to accept Christ are saved, but that the whole world is saved, or is in the process of being saved. These folk believe Jesus when he promised he would draw all to himself (John 12.32). They believe St. Paul when he wrote that all would be made alive in Christ (1 Corinthians 15.22). They believe St. John when he wrote that Jesus was the mercy seat not only for our sins, but the sins of the whole world (1 John 2.2). They believe

Paul's declaration that nothing, not even death, can separate us from the love of God (Romans 8.38-39). They believe that Jesus is an exact showing forth of who the Father is (Hebrews 1.3), and that God is love (1 John 4.8) and wouldn't design a place of torture where most of humanity will spend eternity in agony of the worst kind. They believe that God does indeed punish, discipline, and chastise, us, but His purpose is to correct us, refine us, heal us, and make us mature; indeed, make us like him. And they believe the fire of the age to come is also part of that loving process.

Some people's understanding of Jesus and his work is too small. Jesus and his work are so massive, so towering, so beyond fully comprehending, that our perception of it will always be too small until it includes the redemption of everything and of everyone. We must challenge ourselves to think of Christ re-creating a world where, as Julian of Norwich wrote, "all shall be well, and all shall be well, all manner of things shall be well." And we mustn't fear that such thinking is too much. If anything, it is too little. For Jesus Christ, "is able to do far more abundantly than all that we ask or think." (Ephesians 20)

Indeed, God has raised Jesus from the dead, "and seated him at his right hand in the heavenly places, far above all rule and authority and power and dominion, and above every name that is named, not only in this age but also in the one to come. And he put **all things** under his feet and gave him as head over **all things** to the church, which is his body, the fullness of him who fills all in all." (Ephesians 1.20-23)

Christ's work wasn't to save a handful, but to save everything and everyone the Father placed into his hands, and the Father placed everything and everyone into his hands. "Ask of me, and I make the nations your inheritance, and the ends of the earth your possession," the Father tells the Son (Psalm 2.8). This is what the Son asks of the Father - for the nations, for the ends of the earth. And the Son declares, "And this is the will of him who sent me, that I should lose nothing of all that he has given me, but raise it up on the last day." (John 6.39)

Everyone was made *by* the Son and *for* the Son. And the Son came into this world to seek them out and to save them, and to bring them all into a glorious union with God. "For **by him all things were created**, in heaven and on earth, visible and invisible, whether thrones or dominions or rulers or authorities—**all things were created through him and for him**. And he is before all things, and **in him all things hold together.** And he is the head of the body, the church. He is the beginning, the firstborn from the dead, that in **everything** he might be preeminent. For in him all the fullness of God was pleased to dwell, and through him to **reconcile to himself all things**, whether on earth or in heaven, making peace by the blood of his cross." (Colossians 1.16-20)

Some Christians from the first two camps say to believers from the third camp, "If what you are saying is true, and there is no threat of eternal torment in hell, then why should we be Christians? We're all going to be with God before it's over anyway." But pause for a moment and listen to what is being said. Do we follow Christ just to avoid hell? Is our faith in him just fire insurance? Of course not! We follow him because he is Lord. Because he has defeated sin and death and brings us the life of the world to come in the here and now. We follow him because there is no condemnation in Christ. We follow him because life in this world is better with the Holy Spirit working in our lives. We follow him because we are better people when we do. We follow him because he loves us and we love him.

Christians who embrace such an expansive understanding of Christ's redemptive work are often accused of believing "all religions lead to God," or, "all paths lead to God," or some other such nonsense. Nothing could be further from the truth. Jesus Christ is the way, and no one comes to the Father but through him (John 14.6). No, all roads don't lead to God. But God in Christ will walk down every road there is, in the middle of the darkest and stormiest night, looking for his lost sheep and bringing them home.

And that, my friends, is good news.

A Partial List of Notable Christians Both Ancient And Modern Who Held The Hope That All Should Be Saved

The list is almost endless when it comes to naming early Christians who held to some form of the hope for the salvation of all. Ilaria Ramelli wrote,

"The main Patristic supporters of the *apokatastasis* theory, such as Bardaisan, Clement, Origin, Didymus, St. Anthony, St. Pamphilus Martyr, Methodius, St. Macrina, St. Gregory of Nyssa (and probably the two other Cappadocians), St. Evagrius Ponticus, Diodore of Tarsus, Theodore of Mopsuestia, St. John of Jerusalem, Rufinus, St. Jerome and St. Augustine (at least initially), Cassian, St. Isaac of Nineveh, St. John of Dalyatha, Ps. Dionysius the Areopagite, probably St. Maximus the Confessor, up to John the Scot Eriugena, and many others, grounded their Christian doctrine of *apokatastasis* first of all in the Bible.[8]

Among the most notable of the early church:

Clement of Alexandria, died c. 215: a priest in Egypt, Clement founded the "Alexandrian School" of theology, wrote the first Christian catechetical material, and several other important works. Origen was his student.

---

[8] Ramelli, Ilaria; *The Christian Doctrine of Apokatastasis*, p. 11, Brill, Boston, 2013.

Origen of Alexandria, died c. 253: one of the most influential thinkers in the entirety of Christianity, second perhaps only to Augustine. He was a priest in Egypt and the first true theologian in the Church.

Athanasius, died 373: After being the champion of orthodox doctrine at the Council of Nicea, the deacon Athanasius later became bishop of Alexandria, Egypt.

Diodore of Tarsus, died c. 390: born in Antioch, Diodore served as the bishop of Tarsus and was an instrumental leader at the First Council of Constantinople.

Gregory of Nyssa, died c. 395: the "Father of Fathers," and the bishop who chaired the First Council of Constantinople in 381, personally assisting in crafting the final version of the Nicene Creed.

Theodore of Mopsuestia, died 428: a childhood friend of St. Chrysostom and bishop of the city of Mopsuestia, Theodore was a theologian and leader in the "Antiochian School" of theology.

Peter Chrysologus, died 450: bishop of Ravenna, declared a Doctor of the Church by Rome in 1729.

As the Augustinian school grew in influence, the doctrine of the restoration of all diminished in popularity, but was never snuffed out. Later notable Christians who embraced this teaching include…

Lady Julian of Norwich, died 1416: the 14th century anchoress whose *Revelations of Divine Love* has become a classic of Christian spirituality. "But all shall be well, and all shall be well, and all manner of things shall be well."

William Law, died 1761: an Anglican priest, honored with a feast day in the Anglican Church calendar and author of the classic *A Serious Call To A Devout And Holy Life*.

Thomas O. Allin, died 1909: An Irish born Anglican priest remembered for his book *Universalism Asserted*.

John A.T. Robinson, died 1983: Anglican bishop of Woolwich and noted New Testament scholar.

Hans Urs Von Balthasar, died 1988: Perhaps the most influential modern Roman Catholic theologian, the Swiss born Balthasar was the favorite theologian of Saint John Paul II. His book, **Dare We Hope That All Men Be Saved?** is careful to stay within Roman Catholic doctrinal boundaries, saying that it is impossible to declare categorically that all will be saved, but it is our responsibility as Christians to hope for that very thing.

Madeleine L'Engle, died 2007: noted award winning Anglican author of many children's books, fantasies, and theological reflections, including *A Wrinkle In Time*.

Thomas Talbott: Professor Emeritus of Philosophy at Willamette University, Salem, Oregon, and perhaps the most notable contemporary Protestant theologian known for embracing the hope for the salvation of all. Author of *The Inescapable Love of God*.

Following on the heels of Balthasar, several living theologians of distinction have weighed in supporting the doctrine, including the Orthodox writers Metropolitan **Kallistos Ware**, Metropolitan **Hilarion Alfeyev**, **David Bentley Hart**, and **Brad Jerzak**. Their books are listed in the bibliography.

A Select Annotated Bibliography

Alfayev, Hilarion, *Christ the Conqueror of Hell*, St. Vladimir's Seminary Press, New York, 2009. A magnificent study by a leading Russian Orthodox cleric, this book explores the biblical, patristic, and liturgical insights to Christ descending into Hades and rising as conqueror over death, including an important discussion on the hope that all will be saved.

Allin, Thomas; annotated by Robin Parry, ***Christ Triumphant: Universalism Asserted as the Hope of the Gospel on the Authority of Reason, the Fathers, and Holy Scripture***, Wipe and Stock, London, 2015. Originally published in 1887, this book by an Irish Anglican priest and theologian has been a standard on the subject for over a century.

Balthasar, Hans Urs Von, ***Dare We Hope That All Men Be Saved***, St. Ignatius Press, San Francisco, 2014. Originally published in German in 1986, this book by one of the most significant Roman Catholic theologians in modern history explores the theology, biblical witness and patristic understanding regarding hell, and the hope that God will redeem all souls. A foundational book for the serious student of the subject, but a read that demands careful attention.

Beauchemin, Gerry, ***Hope Beyond Hell***, Malista Press, Olmita, TX, 2007, revised 2016. Written from an Evangelical

Protestant perspective, this book is a thorough introduction to the subject, with scriptural references on nearly every page. A good place to begin digging deeper.

Burnfield, David, ***Patristic Universalism***, self-published, 2016. A slightly misleading title, this book does not delve much into the patristic writings, but is a valuable resource for studying the subject from a philosophical and scriptural perspective.

Hart, David Bentley, ***That All Shall Be Saved***, Yale University Press, New Haven, 2019. Hart, a former high church Anglican and now Orthodox theologian has written a no-holds-barred tour de force book which explores the subject of universal reconciliation with the skill of a biblical exegete, a philosopher, and a first rate theologian.

Jerzak, Brad, ***Her Gates Will Never Be Shut: Hell, Hope, and the New Jerusalem***, Wipf & Stock Publishers, London, 2005.

Jerzak began his ministry and writing as an Evangelical Protestant and has recently entered the Orthodox Church. This book is a fair and straightforward exploration of all the views of hell embraced by Christians throughout history, with a focus on the validity of a hope for the restoration of all.

MacDonald, George, ***Unspoken Sermons***, various editions. Originally published in 1867 this classic collection of sermons offers and in depth and insightful look at the love of God and his intention to restore all to himself. Various editions are available today, including one modernized with today's English, edited by David Mackey. MacDonald was very influential in the spiritual life of C.S. Lewis and G.K. Chesterton.

Ramelli, Ilaria L.E., ***A Larger Hope? Volume One: Universal Salvation from Christian Beginnings to Julian of Norwich***, Cascade Books, Eugene, OR, 2019. Ramelli is the Full Professor of Theology and the K. Britt Chair in Christology at the Graduate

School of Theology, Thomas Aquinas University in Rome. In this, and the subsequent volume (*A Larger Hope?, Volume 2, Universal Salvation from the Reformation to the Nineteenth Century*) Ramelli does a deep dive into the theology and history of the Christian universal salvation doctrine. Perhaps the most scholarly book in this list, and one of significant influence in the current discussion of the subject.

About the Author

Kenneth Myers was born in 1959 in Denison, Texas where he now lives. The son of a pastor/missionary, he was married to Shirley McSorley for 40 years, until her death in 2017. They have three children and five grandchildren. Ken is an Anglican bishop, a traveling teacher leading seminars and retreats around the world through the ministry he calls Graceworks, and the author of 13 books.

www.kennethmyers.net

Made in the USA
Columbia, SC
20 December 2023